The Unheard Story Of Hope: Vol 1

The Unheard Story Of Hope: Vol 1

The Unedited Thoughts & Scribbles Of A Bipolar Aquarius

Dr. Hazel Du'Bois

Published by Tablo

Table of Contents

Dedicated to a few HOPES: 1

Intro: 7

Thoughts & Scribbles   9

Chapter 2: The Winter-Spring Thoughts   11

Bipolar Disorder   19

Chapter 4: The Spring-Summer Scribbles   21

Chapter 6: Summer-Fall Thoughts   25

The Chaotic Aquarius Mind   31

Chapter 8: The Fall-Winter Scribbles (This ish is long   33
IDC if you skip this chapter LOL)

Chapter 10: The Season of Bipolar Thoughts   45

Thoughts & Scribble Sharing Time (use the next few   51
pages to share your thoughts and unedited scribbles my
hope)

Chapter 12: The Season of Bipolar Scribbles   55

ASE' ASE' ASE'   59

Dedicated to a few HOPES:

JB,
Wow! My 1st real loss was loosing you! 2007 slapped the ish out of me if I may take a moment to be honest! I love you blood I miss you so much! Your son is so BIG now such a young man with such a great future. He's a class clown like you smdh always pranking and full of sarcastic remarks. The mini version of you lol! Moms is good as well I am actually really proud of her journey and strides to heal and LIVE! Keep watching over me my War Angel! Missed, Gone But trust me you will NEVER be forgotten! 18 years was not enough but I am confident that you are resting and free of pain!

Tone,
My sweet love how I miss your touch, your smell, you lips, your smile, your laugh! Our souls crossed paths in a math class and from that moment on WE were in love you were my best friend! I cannot believe you left me to walk across that stage to earn our undergraduate degree alone! Man I just knew we would share that moment together, and celebrate afterwards. Thank you for all the times you loved on me, all the times you provided for me, all the times you held me on holidays so we didn't have to be alone! Tone I miss you baby and although our time shared was short I will forever cherish all the memories we shared and all the love moments we had! Can't say it enough I miss you boo I truly do!

Beauty,
My forever valentine I love you! I miss you! I need you! I wish you were here! Life with you was so amazing and now life without you can be so confusing at times. I try daily to stay a float knowing that not even those close to me will ever

understand that when you died I did too. I long to hold you, smell you, feel you, kiss you, breath you. I crave you like honey in my daily tea. Honestly, the past six years of my life have been HELL on earth! I realized that I am in my rebirth season and have to complete this season without you; the one I love now and forever and always. I am really trying Beauty! I know you saw the shit show LOL I guess the grief from loosing you brought out the worst in me but eventually it all turned and is turning into some type of beauty for ashes! Baby just keep watching over me! I will carry, love and cherish you for the rest of my earthly days, and even in the next realm of glory I HOPE to still be loving you! I love you forever and always! Damn I miss you! - Amor

Ma (Dr. Caritha Roybal),
Somedays I wish this REALITY was a dream! I cannot believe your gone! But, daily I still hear you saying Hazel LIVE! So, in my pain, grief, sorrow, frustration, confusion, and hurt I strive to LIVE! You saw my gift and encouraged and charged the prophetic worshipper out of me! Thank you! I love you! I miss you! But, I do find peace knowing you are no longer in pain. I try my hardest to keep my brother and sister uplifted and encouraged! You'd be proud of them both! They are so amazing! It hurts me to see them hurting so badly inside as they are missing you daily! G helps me a lot with them. We got them both covered Ma! We've officially given ourselves a name LOL we call us "The 6" Ma! We love you our Beautiful Angel we miss you more than ever!

Grandma Dickson,
What can I say! For years I was able to just call you and find comfort hearing your voice on the other side of the phone. Our bond was different! You knew me the real me and you didn't care you just covered loved and supported me! Your prayers are

literally what kept me and is still keeping me! I tell everyone that your unconditional love for me was and is irreplaceable. I love you Grandma ill meet you in heaven when my train to glory arrives. PS I'm not rushing it anymore grandma I actually have discovered I have much to live for. I honestly believe you would be proud of me!

Daddy,
the 33rd sunk up on us and took you to the galaxies afar. Boy do I miss our early morning convos. Our dark shared humor expressed by laughing at ish we should be crying about! I have yet to delete your number out of my phone, somedays I just wish I could hear your laugh, visualize your smile and smell ya dolla store cologne LOL Rest My Nig I'll see you on the 33rd. Always your twin.

Ms. Bean,
Its because of you and Yeshua I have life! I am thankful you kept me. I am grateful for our journey (the good, the bad, the pretty, the ugly). Although for years I never truly understood US! I am thankful for the US we now share! I love you Ms. Bean, I appreciate you Ms. Bean, and I am thankful for you Ms. Bean. You are the strongest WOMAN I know I am glad I was taught how to survive and encompass strength as a state of mind.

Mama,
Thank you! Thank you for accepting me! Thank you for uplifting me! Thank you for believing in me! Thank you for supporting me! Thank you for loving me! Thank you for being you for me! I love you forever! Its forever me and you against the odds.

Deion & Geralean,
My siblings! Man! What would life be without you two. Yal have literally been through some of the most pivotal times in my

journey. The bond we have I NEVER want to loose. I admire your strength! I applaud your hustle! I commend you for your dedication to WIN! I love you both so much and I am so thankful for your love, your grace, your loyalty, your encouragement! I'll forever RIDE OR DIE for us THE 6!!

Turtle, Byrd, & MiniMe,
I love you 3 so much! My life would be incomplete without you in it! I want the best for you, we all do! We want you to WIN, & SUCCEED! Yal got this now go be tf great! PS NEVER doubt the love WE have for you all! We are not perfect at this parent thing! We really don't know WTF we doing LOL but we are trying daily to give yal a better life. ensure that you all can be great! we got your back! Yal are our hearts and even when we don't understand each other we are yet growing and will always be FAMILY! THE 6 FOREVER & ALWAYS!

Kayla & My Grands CamBam & Ms.Demi,
Daughter I love you! I'm here! I believe in you! I see past the pain! I desire for you to rise above all the odds you have faced! You got this daughter!
CamBam Grandma Hazel loves you so much my sweet baby boy! Not a day goes by that I do not pray for you.
DemiNicole my sweet babygirl Grandma Hazel loves you so very much!

LadyBug,
My baby brother (LOL) I love you so much! I am proud of you! I am here now, then and always! Big Sis <3

Familia,
You already know what it is! I love you both to the moon and back never doubt or forget that! This is our WINNING SEASON!

Thank you for being who are in my life! I appreciate you, I truly do!

Intro:

Well if you have purchased and opened this long-overdue release of a book; your more than likely curious about my story. So, thanks for your curiosity just know that in the next set of flipped pages I will be expressing my raw, real, bi-polar highs and lows with you LOL.

Life is full of surprises my heart is hopeful that even in the worst of times things must get better. Stay tuned as I begin to share my chaotic world in the most open way with you (sharing my thoughts, my writings, my utopia)! Just call me hopeful as I am The Unheard Story of Hope (Heb 11:1)!

What do I know about HOPE? I'm sure thats what your wondering. Well as a child & what I am about to share with you is all I ever knew about HOPE; **Hebrews 11:1** Now faith is the assurance of things hoped for, the conviction of things not seen. **Romans 15:13** May the God of hope fill you with all joy and peace in believing, so that by the power of the Holy Spirit you may abound in hope.

I was tested, tried in the fire as some ole church motha would say. But, it was in the moments of I can't I learned I could and HOPE was the reason why. You see when I found this meaning of HOPE I discovered it to mean life after death, strength in grief, healing in sickness, peace in chaos, a heart in heartache, a song to a melody, a rainbow at the end of a storm.

My brother Deion (rolling eye emoji) says I sound like a crybaby but honestly it is just my dark humor he doesn't sometime understand when reading my scribbles LOL. If you know me and need to hear my voice to understand something you've read in the pages ahead call me (smiley face).

Anyways cheers to your dying curiosity of what I have to share. I am the Bipolar Aquarius like none you've ever met before. Enjoy this roller coaster. Thanks again for your time!

Thoughts & Scribbles

THOUGHTS....

I thought I wanted a forward or a few forwards from various influences in my life. But, of course my bipolar ask changed my mind when I asked them to write a forward for me they said they needed to read my book first LOL! This makes perfect sense and I completely understand where they were coming from! But, my first thought was they won't understand any of the thoughts and scribbles presented in the next few pages so who needs a forward when you really just wrote a book to share your unedited thoughts pertaining to the Utopia you reside in!

Thanks for taking time out of your busy life to support and read my extremely randomness......I have learned throughout my journey that I am not for everyone! My presence is strong, independent, and often unwelcoming. But, I assure you I love hard. I care hard. I carry hard. I protect even harder. I may not always be the best version of me thanks to my bipolar disorder but I am learning to love all me even if I happen to be the outcast. I love each of you my hopes again you just read some of my random thoughts in a nutshell. This book is not to be understood, it is my way of letting you nosey mfrs jkjk into my world. So, let me introduce you to the real me. Hi I Am Hopeful Hazel currently don't really have a last name LOL I am too cheap to pay to change my name back and honestly I don't live in my past! So, Hopeful Hazel it is!!!!!

SCRIBBLES....

sometimes I love waking up in the mornings sometimes I hate getting out of the bed. sometimes I love going for a walk and being active but sometimes I literally desire to do nothing see no one and go no where. sometimes life makes me happy while other times it breaks me. sometime ago I wanted death until I realized you could be alive and be dead all at the sometime. Kinda like religion and spirituality. ones afraid of going to the hell while the others already been. sometimes I laugh so hard I cry. but sometimes I cry so hard laugh. sometimes I have high hope but sometimes my hope can be low. Ultimately hope is what has carried me and I am hopeful my randomness is relatable or at least entertaining for most!

Chapter 2: The Winter-Spring Thoughts

I BELIEVE IT WAS SOME TIME IN THE BEGINNING OF 2018

A note to 2018 can you please Be Good to Me? Day 2 of 2018… (SOME THOUGHTS & SCRIBBLES) Wow! Can you believe we have entered another year? A year that provides us with another chance to perfect what we have failed at, and another moment to embrace who we are this far.

2018 I have "NO" resolutions, my heart's desire is simple, that I experience an overflow of joy and financial freedom. What does the number 18 mean or represent? I am always thinking deeply in hopes for some profound revelation that will enlighten my path LOL.

Spiritually speaking the number 18 represents a form of bondage but it also represents a healing SEASON. You know the story about the lady who had a 'spirit of infirmity that had her bent over for 18 years, but then Jesus healed her while he was teaching in a Synagogue…. Yeah, that is the type of instantaneous healing I am looking for physically, emotionally, and spiritually throughout the duration of TWO! ZERO! ONE! EIGHT! YEAR!

If I may be a bit dramatic I have felt like the past ten years of my life have been nothing short of a living HELL. The murder of my brother, an epic failure at marriage, the death of my BEAUTY, the loss of my praying grandmother (Grandma Dickson), the death of my spiritual covering (Ma CC), and the fact I have been floating out here with no covering for nearly 2 years now feeling completely lost and alone.

I can only hope that 2018 is truly my healing season. That the solitude I am experiencing brings forth a fountain of faith. That my pain turns into a testimony of strength and endurance and that even in my weakness I grow stronger in all aspects of my life. I am hopeful that I learn to trust again, that I can actually accept real LOVE again and that I do not make the same mistakes I have in my past. When it comes to my well-being! Just call me hopeful as I am the unheard story of hope!

THE POWER OF 3'S DR. JOHN F. HANNAH A PROLIFIC INSPIRATIONAL SPEAKER PROCLAIMED ON SUNDAY, JAN 28TH AT APPROXIMATELY 825A A POWERFUL DECLARATION OVER MY LIFE (I'M AN ONLINE MEMBER LOL), "I DECREE AND DECLARE THAT YOU WILL CATCH SOMETHING HUGE THIS YEAR."

The biblical passage I believe was coming from John 21:6. You know where Jesus decides to appear to the seven disciples, refers to them using the term "friends" (NIV) asking them if they had caught any fish? And they responded with NO. So He then advises them to throw their net out to the "RIGHT" side of their boat informing them that if they obeyed this simple instruction they would find some. So they did and like that instantaneously they were overflowing with fish.

So let's get back to the declaration I made mention of earlier. "I Decree and Declare that YOU will catch something HUGE this year." HUGE? Of course I would begin to ask questions after repeating such a powerful affirmation. What exactly is the HUGE in my life? What does the HUGE mean or represent?

I am now officially 33, divorced, and living in mere devastation (3 years on 2/25/18), several attempt suicide survivor and somewhat still battling an ounce of depression. I'm a workaholic, insomnia battler, grad student at two different schools, studying two different programs at the same time, a skirmish OCD individual who is constantly striving to be something in life, often forgetting I already am SOMEBODY special! Have you ever just got lost inside your own head that it literally overtakes your correlation between the force of good and bad? Leaving you to reflect more on the bad verse the good? This is definitely my daily struggle...

Well numbers have always meant something to me so with Dr. Hannah's declaration and God allowing me to live to see the big 33 I could only wonder if the HUGE would intertwine with the 3's I now carry with me for an entire year in my journey. The number 3 spiritually speaking refers to the Trinity, that one will receive divine protection, help and guidance. The more 3's you see is a sign of an Angelic connection and closeness to Jesus. 33 meaning that Jesus is with you and helping you. The more 3's (333) you see indicates some sort of HUGE message.

As I am still not sure what the HUGE is in my life I am only hopeful that it will allow me to grow stronger, wiser and better. That I will think before I respond and speak. That I will listen to the provided guidance before making an irrational decision. That will I tap into my purpose and that I am able to help others as my soul desires. I can only hope that the HUGE will allow me to get lost in myself with love for life and a passion to live in truth. That the HUGE will be a representation of the 3's in my life bringing meaning to my heartache but healing to my future.

For the remaining of this year and honestly maybe even into the next I will strive to remind myself that something HUGE no matter what I face is happening in my life!

H.I.M.

I cried aloud to H.I.M. a plea to be rescued, a scream from my soul that only he would be able to comprehend. In hopes that he would save me from myself. I'm on a path of self destruction, I'm trapped in a cloud of depression and my darkness has now become my light. I'm in desperate need of H.I.M. right now. To hear me, comfort me, and uplift me. He is the only one who can do the things I need to be done in my life. In this moment I'm entirely lost and I need H.I.M. like I've never needed H.I.M. before. But will he come through or am I going to be the lost soul who could only hope in H.I.M. and never experience the abundance he holds. In H.I.M. I once found safety and place of peace. Not sure who left who or how we've become so distant.

My only hope is that he sees me and will restore me back to a place in H.I.M. where even I know I belong.

H.E.R. (1998.15.03)

My prayer for H.E.R. is that this be the start of greatness in H.E.R. life! That H.E.R. mind be sound and filled with only good thoughts about H.E.R. self and who she is becoming. That she never doubt H.E.R. self or the magnitude of excellence that she can reach and will reach! That she boldly becomes knowledgeable of H.E.R. anointing. That she recognizes that she is equipped to be and make a difference. That she believe confidently in H.E.R. self as she has been empowered to lead and not follow. That God guides all of H.E.R. thoughts daily. And no matter what comes H.E.R. way she never forgets that there is no obstacle she cannot overcome as she has been destined for VICTORY! Everything she needs lies within H.E.R. *I still wish you well Angel! - Amor*

ACKNOWLEDGE AND GROW

Often times we get comfortable in the baby stages of our lives. We fall apart when things go wrong, we complain about bills, how others have or are treating us, we become victims to the concept of dead growth. When in all reality growth is a developmental process that cannot exist if it is not properly nourished. What do I mean by that? I'm glad you asked well when a gardener is planting the end process is that what is to bloom will be beautiful. The same thing goes for our lives. We must acknowledge what has been planted inside of us; the dreams, the gifts and so forth and then take the necessary steps to watch them blossom. If we do not take the proper steps as a gardener would do by watering the seeds that were planted. No growth will transpire. But when steps have been successfully complete full growth can be established. Where we are now is not the end there's more to our growth process. Don't allow a dry season in your life to be a drag sentence. Acknowledge you areas of weakness, applaud your strengths, and continue to water you growth process with positive thoughts and vibes! #UnheardHope #JustCallMeHopeful

Pain

This impromptu iPhoneX photoshoot (courtesy of My brothers phone). Snapped by my amazingly talented toxic lover (at that time) was beyond an exciting day. Linked up and attended a Cannapreneur event. And for a short moment, I felt carefree, worry free, and safe. I felt like I belonged to something like I mattered and was important! Like no one was judging me for being me. But the smile witnessed in these photos has been hidden behind my pain, my past, my setbacks, my disappointments, my frustrations, my struggles, and even my desire/s to quit. Have you ever been in a stage of your life when nothing goes right? Not even putting a knife to your wrist? If so you will get where I am coming from. Mentally I've been a volcanic eruption just waiting to explode. Shit after shit keeps piling up and NOW I literally cannot breathe. No sad story just truth as everybody reaches a breaking point and I'm taking this moment to share that I'm at mines! I'm sick of helping people and getting F'd over! Sick of supporting people who only complain! Tired of being strong for everyone and when my back is against the wall my reach, and vision is out to a ghost! No one can be found, or really understands! Yes, I have my mother, brother, my person, little sister, nephew, and sons! But inside I feel so lost and alone! I can't express to them how I feel as they don't truly understand where I'm coming from. Mental health is real, depression is an overtaker, and the demon of suicide always manages to make things seem like the right route. I'm not sharing my TRUTH for pity today, or for your opinion of my weakness. I'm sharing to say that you truly never know where someone is in life. I've wanted to die since 2015. And for whatever reason, I'm still here! Seeking HELP! So if someone is reading this post today, and has felt or feels like I do; I urge you to seek help, you're not alone, mental health matters, and even when you feel alone your not! A smile can hide a million broken pieces. But today behind the smile in these pictures lies a broken woman, who's been lost for years in hopes of eventually being restored. Just call me hopeful. I am the unheard story of Hope!

Bipolar Disorder

To me this disorder looks like a volcanic explosion! A devastating loss! A train wreck! A plane crash at times! The end of the world! The lack of HOPE & FAITH! The thoughts of suicide! The consumption of liquor. Fights in the streets! A night in jail! Glass shattered and pieces of glass in a hand from a broken window! A 3 day bus ride to Ohio! Marriage & Divorce! Fear of leaving the room! A hatred for people. A lost soul! A forbidden fruit. It feels like strep throat. Pulmonary Fibrosis. Fear of tomorrow. Childhood trauma. A widow experience. The feeling and sound of a heart when it stops beating! The pain of grief. Death with breath. Domestic violence victim and the victor. A house fire. Abandonment, rejection, addiction and so much. But, the disorder also feels like a breeze of fresh air, peace in chaos, HOPE for tomorrow, a blank mindset, merit of existing with no true understanding or knowledge of a purpose. Divine connection. Purpose over passion. Destiny over desire. Surviving the flame. Messages in the smoke and of course so much more....

Waiting To Excel 30 Meditation & Manifestation Zen
Celebration Manifesting a Life of Wealth Namaste -
Deyonwho (You'll Know His Name REAL Soon...)

Chapter 4: The Spring-Summer Scribbles

REFLECTING BACK ON 07/17/17

7/17/17 roughly 330a PST the call I expected unexpectedly came through. I felt it, I saw it, I knew it. Something I've always ignored a secret gift I have often tried to run from. But when death knocks my body is consumed with an array of chills and a glimpse of white clouds hosting a smile of my loved ones face. Back to the call: on the other end as I answered there was no hello all I could say was she's gone. G in disbelief that I knew the reason for her call without her even saying a word. Just asked if my brother had called? My response no, but where is he? Life without you Ma has been different. Some days easier than others. I will never understand why your journey was cut short but I will forever believe in your short time you LIVED your life to the fullest. No words can even express the void of emptiness we each feel with out the warmth of your presence. Only thing that somewhat eases the pain is knowing you are no longer in any form of pain. We love you Ma rest on our Angel. We will see you again. In the garden you so often visit baby Sister in. Until then keep dancing and singing to the rhythm of your own beat. As normal Ma don't worry about us. We don't mind waiting on the Lord to heal us completely of every ache we have endured from loosing you, our jewel. What you have taught us we carry daily and your spirit often convicts us. We love you beautiful and we miss you. One year without you and our lives have and will forever be changed

That One Saturday
Drifting in the battlefield of my mind. So consumed with the pressures of this world, longing for an escape. Be my escape baby. Hold me, grip me, rub me, feed my soul with your

knowledge and wisdom. Ignite the fire of passion since my flame has been deemed out. Restore my jubilance with vibrant colors. Love me back to life. - Self

The Last One (Completion Assignment) JK

Today is the start of my last (JK) MDiv. residency program. And I tell you it's been quite a journey. No real spiritual mentors, no guidance, no one to sow into me, and I've managed to quit religion and become a TRUE believer (NOW OMNIST). Life has a way of awakening your soul. Allowing you to see the inside of a person verse just the outside. It has a way of introducing you to this walk, this journey your on. Presenting the highs and lows and the in betweens. It will either break you or make you. Many times I've desired to quit, walk away from my goals, and even give up on my dreams. But being here now I've shown myself my endurance and that I have will power. I've proven to myself that even in the worst of times I still have a passion to accomplish and complete what I've started. During this program journey I've lost more than I could've imagined. Death on all aspects from lives of my loves, to toxic associations mistaken for friendships. But through it all I'm here, still standing even in the struggle. I'm yet hopeful for more, and I strongly believe this cannot be the end of my journey. I've said all this to say that even when we feel like life is unfair, and we loose sight of our purpose. Don't ever give up on your dreams, or goals. There's always LIGHT at the end of the tunnel. What's for you is for you and what's not well let it be. Live, learn, love and grow. The journey was never promised to be easy but I'm hopeful enough for us all that it will be worth it. A prayer for me today: Dear Most High I pray that during this residency that I AM healed, restored, and truly experience a fresh wind of God. I pray that YOU FATHER birth new life into me and allows me to forget, and forgive what I've been facing. Forgive me of all my shortcomings. I truly desire to become NEW.

WASHINGTON, DC

The crisp humid air, the life slept on the streets, the sound of the trumpet as I walked through history. The robust of the wind, the refreshing tears of God. Washington your history rings a sound of hope, and dreams back into the lost soul of ones grieving heart. Thank you clouds of sunshine for restoring jubilance back into me. The truth is I'm just a hopeful gal full of passion who refuses to settle for the bullshit she once accepted. I got a lost a little but trust and believe I've been found

#UnheardHope #HopefulHazel #iAm #TheUnheardStory #OfHope #locsroc #GirlsWithLocsRoc #LocJourney #iLoveMyLocs #iBlog #BloggerLife #MyStory #MyJourney #MyWorld #MyUtopia #SeeThroughMyEyes

U STREET
METRO STATION
Washington, DC

Chapter 6: Summer-Fall Thoughts

SCHOOL TIME FOR THE 3

So, It's that time of the year again. You know when summer vacation has to come to an end and our children for the most part are advancing to another grade level. As a parent, or guardian you feel a sudden burst of excitement for this change. The freedom of having some privacy again, a fridge full of food, and possibly some extra money as this amazing little person we love won't be begging for everything they see on TV or the internet, or the stupid gaming system (fortnite) LOL. But, truth is I am eager for their opportunity to learn, explore and expand their mind comprehension. As life is all about learning.

So, I pray that when they are not in our care what we've taught them and have been made to feel that they have ignored is actually a sign of active listening and shown as effective outside of our presence. I pray that no child get so upset with anyone or by anything that causes them to want to bring harm to the campuses we've left our children on. I pray that the teachers have patience, love, and compassion for each of our children we are trusting them with throughout the week. I pray that our children respect, appreciate, listen, and assist each of the teachers they come in contact with. I pray that they understand that

CHARACTER MATTERS, that RESPECT IS EARNED, that TRUST IS BUILT, and that LIFE IS ALL ABOUT LEARNING.

I pray that they do better in their academics than they did the year before. I pray that nightly they come home excited to share what they learned. I pray that they say NO to drugs, sex, gangs, bullying, alcohol, disrespectful behavior, inappropriate conversing, and anything that they already know we wouldn't support or encourage. I pray that they take their education/ academic seriously. I pray they realize this is not a JOKE! I pray they see how hard we work and how much we want better for them and strive to be GREAT daily.

I pray for our children <3

PAYDAY FRIDAY HAS ARRIVED

that very moment of numbness that I knew change had arrived. Was it a change I desired, a change I dream't of or a change I was prophetically required to experience? Either or it was here and my proclamation of exhilaration was no longer non-existent but factual. So, I smiled no longer to keep from crying. Laughed no longer did I feel I was dying. But, for that moment I finally felt whole. My bank account was welcoming on a payday Friday ." – UnheardHope
#HopefulHazel

"THE 33RD"

As a child my father used to always tell us he would see us on the 33rd, or he bring us money on the 33rd or he be back on the 33rd. Whatever it was we often would be waiting, longing, and looking forward to the 33rd. Of course my dear sweet mother had to burst our bubble of hope and let us know that the how irrelevant the 33rd was and how the 33rd didn't exist and that he (to refrain from vulgar wording) LOL wasn't coming! Wow! As I reminisce on that memory shared between my father my siblings I would've never thought that the 33rd would be relevant.

My father didn't raise me, missed out on almost all of my life moments! But, when he did show up boy the joy it brought my soul. I longed for a lifetime to be daddy's little girl. What girl doesn't dream of having her daddy tuck her in at night, protect her from harm, escort her to high school formals, or even walk her down the aisle? Although I never experienced or shared that with my father I do know we had an unusual bond. Some sort of unique bond that even in our disagreements we rendered **LOVE**. It took me years to release the anger I held towards him. For not being there when I felt and believed he as my father should've been.

MOMENT OF TRUTH

I was molested at 3 months and my thoughts are where was my father? I was rapped at 15 and my thoughts again where was my father? I was mentally, physically, and verbally abused and again where was my father? I was living on my own at 16, and dating men entirely older than me, yet again and where was my father? Our baby brother Joshua was brutally murdered March 1st of 2007. We called our father in such despair, and tremendous grief begging him to get to us. He never showed. It took me literally up until after the funeral service for expression "the 33rd" to become literal to me. When he didn't show up to his own sons funeral and could only say he couldn't bury his son; he wasn't ready! Is when I knew he just couldn't be....AND since he couldn't I HAD to forgive, accept, and love him for who he was regardless of who I wanted and desired him to be to and for me. I'm not even sure if that makes sense.... any who I remember leaving the repass, parting ways with my grieving mother, and siblings and going home.

I decided to pickup the phone and call my father. I wept like a baby on the phone and begged his forgiveness for hating him, and for blaming him for everything he couldn't be in my life. For the first time in my entire life I saw my father vulnerable, heard him break, cry, weep, sob. I could feel his hurt, hear his pain, and accept his love, and I knew he truly just didn't know how to be that to me or any of my siblings. For years we have had distance. We may of never been as close as I'd like for us to be but, we spoke weekly. I mailed cards, even had got into the habit of sending Father's Day goodies and cards to make sure he knew how important he was in my life. Although it had been roughly twelve years since we actually seen one another smelled one another or even touched one another.

It was Monday October 15 when I got a random snap chat message form my baby sister asking if I had heard from my brother about my dad. I tried to call his phone no answer so I frantically called my grandpa of course his 90 year old ask ain't no nothing LOL. I finally got in touch with my siblings and was informed our dad was on life support. His heart stopped Sunday the October 14th literally a month after his 61st birthday and he was brain damaged. The doctors several of the informed us that he was not going to return to us. That he was a vegetable, and that is when we decided to let him go. He least told us if he couldn't whip his own ass let him go. One of the hardest decisions I've ever had to make and trust I've made a few. I flew into town on Tuesday October 16th went straight from the airport in an Uber the hospital to see my dad. I was consumed with so many emotions, so many thoughts traveling through my mind along that ride.

I got there and just held his hand. I could see he was suffering, and was in pain. I was a little upset that he didn't tell me he was really sick. I knew he was sick I just truly thought I had time to see him. He trusted me with his affairs I was his POA funny right. The one who couldn't one find time to visit was the one he knew could handle all final arrangements when push came to shove. I work so much, work so hard and hate to struggle but after losing my daddy I've learned time waits for no one. And memories can't be created when your just focusing on paying bills.

On Wednesday October 17th at 122p our daddy gained his wings. And just like that I'm graced I guess we can call it that to watch life leave someone else I love. I've seen life come into the world but watching it exit has been something I just have not been able to process (pray for me). For my family I held a small service that Saturday (10/20) so we could say our goodbyes to our father, their uncle, their brother, grandpas sons. Thank God for my spiritual parents coming to my rescue and being my strength.

Idk what I would've done if PJ wouldn't of been there preaching heaven down, and Mamas sweet melodic voice sending comfort to our souls. When I entered into ministry my father was so proud he was once licensed reverend amongst the baptist faith. I would mail him videos of the different times I was blessed to minister the the people of God. So I MC'd his service, I wanted to celebrate his life have some church he was a praiser for reals and true man who feared and loved God. One who repented daily and never was embarrassed to admit he often feel short.

PJ preached a powerful word out of Job 23:1-10 "The Trail Is Over". Sunday (10/21) I flew home wept on two different planes, Monday (10/22) couldn't get out the bed, Tuesday (10/23) went back to work attempting to act like nothing happened, and pretending I was good! Ultimately I wasn't good, honestly I'm still not good I've just become one who truly knows how to keep going no matter what.

I know I started with how irrelevant the 33rd was but ironically it must've been one of my dads favorite numbers or something. His address had 33 in it, he died literally 33 days after his birthday and to top it off 3 of his kids are exactly 33 in this present moment. So cheers the the 33rd and whatever it holds or represents. Here it is Wednesday 11/7 I'm laid up in the hospital blood pressure sky high, yet consumed with my emotions but still hopeful that even in all of my grief something BIG is bound to happen in my LIFE. I had serval losses especially over the course of the pst 3 years. Things have happened that have caused setbacks for setups, betrayal for loyalty, sorrow for triumph, heartache for hope, confusion for peace, and most importantly separation to bring me back to God. We all face tons of.

Some days it piles up and life just feels like a blur. But even when we want to quit we can't. Someone needs OUR strength. I didn't know how strong I was until being strong was all I knew. Prayers are needed yes please, but most importantly remind me that I m stronger than I feel if you don't mind. I love you thanks for reading this long butt blog

I love you Daddy rest well sir peace out I'm gone as you often would say (In memory of Rev. Horace Lee Mims Jr.) 9/14/61 - 10/17/18 life is short we must truly learn to LOVE if we lack love we have not learned to LIVE

The Chaotic Aquarius Mind

Eccentric, energetic, shy, in my head type of deep thinking. Visualizing tomorrow, confused about today and lost in what the future may hold. A piece of peace but a bliss of panic after a suppressed hurricane. Chaotic! Direct with no filter. Emotionless or over emotional. Hard to read but easy to love. Over-thinker! High Intuition (a prophetic gift)!

420 Celebration on El Cajon Blvd San Diego 2017

Chapter 8: The Fall-Winter Scribbles (This ish is long IDC if you skip this chapter LOL)

HAPPY 31ST BIRTHDAY

It's was November 12, 1988. Our mother gave birth to you. Instantly my mind mentality changed from singleness to partnership. I instantly began to think of you every time I ate, drank or went somewhere. What I got you needed as well. What I wanted I knew you had a want or a need. My selfish desires became selfless as my focus was on two instead of one early on in life. I became a protector, a provider, a defender, a mentor, a leader, a big sister. You looked you to me and I never wanted to disappoint you or let you down in anyway. To this day I hope I made you proud. Now as time and age managed to entwine between us we didn't always agree. But one thing for sure is we were natural "RIDERS" for each other!

Our scoop on life was different yet so similar. We care/cared for people, help/helped people and defended those of weaker stance more often than we probably should. The cause of your death is evident of the person, the "RIDER" you were! I love you, thank you for leaving us your son. Mekhi is literally my life, my pride my joy, and one of my reasons I keep striving to be better daily. He's so much like you it's annoying at times LOL his sense of humor, he's such a jokester, and he's def a ladies man smdh but ultimately his truly a great kid! I never imagined life without you. But, now that it's reality I guess I've learned to accept it. Acknowledge you as my battle angel.

Find comfort in knowing that for whatever reason God
needed you sooner than we wanted to let you go. Happy 31st
birthday Blood. Your presence is missed. Your laugh is still
heard. Your smile I still see. I love you baby brother I always
have and I always will. There's not a day that will pass where
you don't cross my mind. As I always say rest well blood I got
our moms and your son. Keep watching out for your Mekhi.
I'm trying to teach him to be a respectful young man/man.
I'm trying to teach him that the streets ain't nothing but
trouble. I'm trying to teach him that God is everything and
without him life ain't. I'm not perfect but no one is daily
brother all I do is try to be better for your son! We love you
King take rest.

DISPARITY OF REALITY

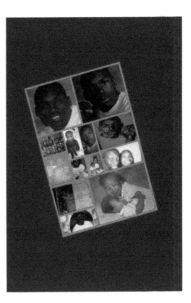

*I am weary, wounded, broken,
hurting, lost, confused, angry,
bitter, frustrated, hated,
unforgiving, empty, lacking,
disturbed, a forbidden cast away,
forgotten*

*But I AM also surviving, standing,
hoping, praying, loving, growing,
learning, focused, manifesting,
longing, loved, forgiving, whole,
abundant, healed, filled, accepted,
desired, thought of, forgiven,
healing*

Just Me & You Just Us Two -
Tupac

*The lessons of life have taught me a
variety of things. My heart has an emptiness so deep that only the*

Messiah can reach. My vision is blurry from the disparity of abuse I have survived. My mind is discombobulated by the confusion of reality. My thoughts are surrounded by Psalm 23:4, "Even though I walk through the darkest valley, I will fear no evil, for you are with me; your rod and your staff, they comfort me.

" My body longs to collapse in the arms of a trusted soul. My soul searches for rest and peace in the soul of a trusted God. My lips speak of Psalm 121. While my spirit yearns for comfortability with a passion that vividly expresses the manifesting of freed soul.

#YeshuaWalks #WithMe #YeshuaTalks #WithMe #YeshuaTellsMe #IAm #HisOwn #YeshuaKeepsMe #YeshuaSavesMe #YeshuaCoversMe #YeshuaGives #MeHope #YeshuaDelieversMe #YeshuaProtectsMe #YeshuaCarriesMe

Finale Today is the final day to release all toxins. What do I mean by this you ask. Well since 12/12/2020 was the final full moon in this current decade we as individuals have had the opportunity to release. Release pain, release bitterness, release anger, release unforgiveness, release hurt, release abuse, release any and everything even people and relationships that have meant us no good.

ALL OF YESTERDAY I HELD BACK TEARS THAT FOR SOME REASON WANTED TO FALL FROM MY EYES. I WAS OVERWHELMED WITH EMOTION, CONSUMED WITH FORGIVENESS AND OPEN TO THE BRIGHT SOVEREIGNTY OF THE HORIZON SURROUNDING THE THOUGHT/S OF A NEW DECADE. WOW! I'M HONESTLY NOT SURE IF I FEEL RELIEVED OR EXCITED FOR THE ENDLESS POSSIBILITIES OF AN ACTUAL NEW BEGINNING IN ALL ASPECTS OF MY FUTURE!

BUT, I DO KNOW FOR SURE THAT I AM BEYOND HOPEFUL THAT MY LESSONS LEARNED IN THIS DECADE HAVE STRENGTHENED ME AND TAUGHT ME A THANG OR TWO SO I NEVER REPEAT ANY SEASONS OF MY NOW KNOWN PAST. I'M HOPEFUL THAT YOU MY HOPES WILL RELEASE TODAY AND BE OPEN TO THE NEWNESS THAT IS COMING WITH YOUR NEW DECADE AS WELL.

HAPPY BORN DAY CHRIST & MAY BLESSINGS OVERTAKE AS YOU ENTER THE A NEW DECADE. MY PRAYER FOR US TODAY IS THAT WE RELEASE TODAY. THAT WE ARE FREED TODAY. GROW TODAY. GLOW TODAY. & RECOVER ALL TODAY. TODAY IS A NEW DAY WITH ENDLESS POSSIBILITIES FOR YOU TO ENCOUNTER THE START OF YOUR NEW BEGINNING. THE QUESTION IS WHAT WILL YOU CHOSE TO DO WITH YOU NEW?

DECEMBER 4TH, 2019

My heart hurts! Our bond was by far something unique. Because of him I was once able to walk in my prophetic calling. Because of him I can verbally say I have a ministry foundation. Because of him I was once a WOG who was a force to reckon with. Because of him I was able to define my relationship with Christ in such a way that I can't verbally explain as there are not enough words in the English dictionary to project the merit connection I was had with Christ. Hearing of his passing brings me to tears, and now there's another void in my heart of emptiness. We've fussed, cussed, cried, laughed, preached, sang, danced, defended one another and supported each other despite our fallouts. We were family he was my brother, my leader, my Bishop before the actual title was given! We loved each other strongly. Didn't always see eye to eye as he often said I was his rebel. But, even with me resigning and walking away from ministry to deal with grief, brokenness, my physical health and my mental health we still spoke from time to time. I Don't think anyone understands that I was young. So I allowed my heart to make decisions for me in a season of vulnerability that affected my natural stance. I felt betrayed, neglected misunderstood, judged and forgotten by a church I poured and gave my all to during the exodus of my 20s and the emotional reality entering my 30s (which have consisted of nothing but grief, neglect and sorrow). We both were broken, hurt, and struggling to make the best of whatever season it is we were facing. Unlike him being surrounded by fake church folks with their prestige's titles wasn't working for me anymore so I disappeared. In more ways than others he was stronger than me when it came to that. I've always been one to avoid fake. My spiritual father taught me in a bible study series you MUST love everyone but you also can DISLIKE someone and I've never forgotten that lesson. I love everyone and theirs a few especially in my misery of San Diego I strongly dislike amongst the "so called" body of Christ. I don't remember the day or the exact time. But, after "The Real" bible study session on a Wednesday night we entered into the sanctuary and heard of an ocean baptism. I immediately signed my entire youth group up including myself, my sons, my daughter and grandkids. We all could use a "re-dip". The moment was priceless. Something so surreal one I'll NEVER forget. Each of us cried like babies snot and all at the fact that we really were making a conscious decision to rededicate, revamp this walk, rekindle the flame of revival that needed to be awakened in us. while for some us it is still lasting and for some of us we've fallen off the wagon it was yet a remarkable step in our Christ walk and salvation journey. He knew I was hurting and he told me he just didn't know how to help. I loved him for his honesty in that moment. For his approach and for his apologetic response when he knew he had possibly wronged someone. I will forever cherish every experience we shared brother/my leader/my pastor/ my forever Bishop. I love you sir I knew you loved me and I am thankful for you and what you were in my life. The good the bad the highs and the lows we carried each other. He often reminded me in our separation that we were family. I appreciate his push. His prayers. His love. His loyalty. His support especially when I lost Beauty. The McCalebs and the New Beginnings Cathedral stood by me no judgement (much curiosity) but tons of love and support. Thank you for your sovereign role in my life. Thank you for birthing my ministry. Thank you for believing in me. Thank you for push. Thank you for calling forth my gifts. Thank you for introducing me to in-depth study of the Word of God. Thank you for challenging me to dig deeper. Thank you for trusting me. Thank you for embracing my rebel Christ-like mentality. Thank you for loving my stubborn ask. Thank you! I love you and I will miss you sir. Take rest. I will see you again.

My Heart Desires PEACE
What a year! 2018 brought about so many peaks and valleys. Made the last payment on my car and then it was wrecked with my child in it, I got sick NUMEROUS times, lost my father, stopped communicating with my boys, my character was sabotaged by the very ones who vowed loyalty to me, and I was literally in the FIGHT of my life. When I stop, and reflect I am blown away by the variation of life changing events that have occurred over the course of nearly four years.

Someday's I believe I am strong, but then of course there are days' depression sinks in and I literally drown in my sorrows. Throughout the course of 2018 I learned a lot about relationships, so I took the initiative to start rediscovering myself. My heart's desire then, and now is to re-identify my IDENTITY as a VICTOR and not a VICTIM.

2019 has just started chapter two of twelve has just begun and the wind is already blowing loudly at me for change and the need to make the changes that will not only enhance me but save me from the earthquake that lies ahead! It all started with an epiphany moment I had in December. It was like I suddenly experienced an awakening that shook the very essence of my soul.

Creating a newness within me that was longing for something that had been missing for years. So, I decided to change things up! Instead of me being the holiday host I took my mother to LA for Christmas (her first time ever, she loved every second of it). Rekindled a connection with a friendship that I've been blessed with for nearly twelve years, and literally just realized that life is meant to be enjoyable. While at work on the 31st of December I decided to DECLARE that this season of grief, depression, anxiety that has consumed me was OVER!!

Boy, why would I say that out loud lol... I then realized that some of the very one's closet to me were the ones' I needed to escape from. Recently while visiting my therapist I went on a well needed, and deserved rant of how sick of being responsible for everyone I am. I informed my therapist that I'm sick of being a provider, a care-taker, a way maker for grown ass people. Who only want MORE from me but never do anything to better themselves.

I feel no guilt for finally proclaiming that it is time for ME to live. In all honesty, I'm at a stage in my life where I truly DGAF who don't like what I do or me for that matter. I have vowed to myself to take the steps needed to make sure I always come first in my life for now on. The goal is to see if I can meet people who will honor, respect and cherish the very depths of my friendship, courtship, and sisterhood. For years, I have been the crumbs to those around me and made to feel of less value while valuing those I hold dear to my heart. Well that shit ends now! I am committed to matching ENERGY (in my brother's voice) LOL

I've learned recently that love stories are merely love fantasies. Yes, love exist so don't think I am speaking against it, as I have had my share of love, and love loss. I just am realizing that love is not control, demand, or pain. It's an intricate sense found in safety, security, provision, and hope that another soul can divinely connect with you soul, and vibe with your vibe. My love story has always been complicated. So, dear future lover if you want me, you must be willing to accept all of me, as I will do the same for you.

I am not a needy person, don't ask for a lot from anyone as I realize the things I desire I can get and do for myself. Honestly, I have spent the first 4 years of my 30's-desiring peace and it's been a complete shit show. Hey, I get stronger every day! I don't know about you but how often should you have to repeat your hearts desires to the very ones who should know you best? For me when the repeating keeps occurring I grow disconnected, uninterested, and entirely uninvolved.

When I reach this stage, there is honestly no turning back I'm done. No hard feelings my loyalty doesn't stop or end. I just build a wall that none of your excuses can bring down ever again! This is often when I begin to experience the betrayal of life. You know that moment/s when the knife is being stabbed in your back by the very one you are waking up to daily, or the one you trust the most with your life. I know I am not the only one who's lived this nightmare as a reality. Funny thing is this happens to be scary; after a while you somewhat get used to this manipulation, schizophrenic behavior mechanism that other use against you for not being who you once were to them. It suddenly becomes your fault that they were unable to meet your needs or your wants or even hear the very cry of your soul!

I am sick of being frustrated, angry, hurt, broken and down due to the unexpected events of life. My goal for now on is to love me back to life. I am choosing me above all as a MFN factor and I refuse to apologize for doing so. I have been guilty of a lot of things but this by far will not be something I feel bad about or allow anyone to make me feel I am wrong for doing. Hazel matters, and saying that out loud actually feels good. So now I embrace chapter 34, I have no idea what the future holds, or where exactly I am heading but I am ready, and committed to living my best got damn life! I'm ready for adventures, new relationships, new experiences, and most of all a new mindset.

Although I will never understand the cards I have been dealt, I am equipped to continue to write my story through this journey no matter what I may face. I am HERE for it, not with the SHITS but READY to conquer whatever obstacles chapter 34 holds with depths of postive and passionate fire.

Day 7 of 2020

Today is the 7th day of the New Year. We are officially 168 hours into a new decade there are 358 days remaining in this season. Have you stopped and truly thought what your focus "word" will be for 2020? Have you taken a moment to ponder on what your true desires are or what you truly want to begin to do or work on this year? Have you spent any time discovering the various areas that may or do need vast improvement in your life; possibly challenged yourself to begin to work on those weaknesses? Are you thinking of your future? Planning for the next decade (10 years) of your life? If these questions spark your thoughts process I dare you today to spend 30 minutes or so with a clear and open mind to dig deeper. Think about past dreams and visions that have yet to come to pass. Fresh start season is never a bad thing Think of

what you would like to do. Write the vision and manifest it. I challenge us to think boldly throughout 2020. We can proclaim that no matter what we are walking in divine favor. Yes, Life is unpredictable but it truly is okay to have a plan, a dream, a desire, a goal, a want, and more for yourself. Let the manifesting begin!

#TheStoryOfUnheardHope #HopefulHazel #YesThatsMe #Thinking #Planning #Discovering #Equipping #Developing #Dreaming #Reality #Focused #Determined #Evolving #Ready #Set #Go #10YearPlan

Chapter 10: The Season of Bipolar Thoughts

2.2.2020

I AM gracefully perfected flawed imperfections. Established February 2nd 1985. How can I explain the pain endured as I'm often lost of words. Even at my weakest my strength is the depths of perseverance.

1. I AM survivor
2. I AM protector and protected by the Messiah
3. I AMdaughter of glowing growth
4. I AM humble reflections
5. I AM birth of unique purpose
6. I AM a prophetic worshipper 7. I AM taught and teacher of wisdom 8. I AM follower of peace as I lead as a peacemaker
9. I AM victor not a victim
10. I AM lover of laugh
11. I AM a healed healer
12. I AM soul divine
13. I AM life after death
14. I AM aligned passion
15. I AM a filtered conjunction
16. I AM the epitome of feminine beauty
17. I AM Ma/Mom/Auntie/Sister/Cousin
18. I AM ready and open to receive love and render love
19. I AM success personified
20. I AM a fearlessly bold
21. I AM fighter for wealth as I'm the lender not the borrower
22. I AM conquer not conquered
23. I AM endured strength
24. I AM safe in the arms of Jehovah Rapha
25. I AM double entendre
26. I AM living proof of bound excellence

27. I AM a driven force

28. I AM a world changer like Harriet Tubman delivered from bondage and slavery of my mind, soul, and spirit

29. I AM freedom freed freely

30. I AM confident that my tests are testimonies that will save other

31. I AM actions to the plan of my life

32. I AM a custom made in and imagine of superior force I AM stronger daily

33. I AM still standing

34. I AM hopeful

35. I AM The Uheard Story of Hope

A prayer for Hazel; that you allow God to take your misery and turn into your ministry. Something "BIG" is about to take off in your life. Don't give up girl you got this! When it's cloudy don't doubt contend for the faith. Your greatness has yet to be witnessed or experienced. What didn't kill you made you stronger. Rise beauty your Lazarus season is over you must LIVE. Know that you are winning! May the Martha in you proclaim boldly Jeremiah 29:11. I decree that the Peter in you embraces love; leans towards a passionate understanding and acceptance knowing you are a forgiving, and forgiven person. May the Noah in you drink classy and less. May the Jonah in you STOP running away but run to the Messiah. May the Thomas in you die so you no longer doubt yourself or the work of Christ in you. May the Sarah in you become so patient and determined. May the Elijah in you become clam and soft spirited. And may you grasp Abrahamic wisdom with each new year.

FRIDAY THE 13TH

Ironically it was Friday the 13th. I had taken a moment to help
something I often do. Well this specific type of help required me
attending a church service. For a while now I've been going
when I can (so many excuses why I can't) to a small lil church
not to far from my home. Oddly enough with every religion I'm
starting to now see some sort of ritual practices will always take
place. They will have some sort of annual/quarterly meeting.
Like a checkup a moment for all to gather and just share, fellow-
ship (don't worry I know it's one word, it will make sense later I
promise).

So, of course I'm late. Purposely late I allowed a lil friend I got
come over before my "outing" we of course could of postponed
that but hey I'm Living My Best Free Life" and figured a lil
hanging wouldn't hurt anything. So, my lil friend leaves, when
she does I head out. Knowing it will take me roughly 15-20
minutes to get there. As I'm driving the Pastor texts my phone.
My thoughts oh shit she cares. Not fully honest but not
completely lying I respond with I'm down the street. Which I
was but I was completely down the street like 5-6 more lights
down the street

I finally made it their Bishop was up giving his tutorial on the
topic of kingdom-ship. The tools needed to build and maintain
kingdom-ship. Well after his tutorial/TED talk he called
everyone up for prayer (location: the front of the church and
altar). Ugh, I think to myself I mean I have on joggers and lose
fitting sweater with uggs (you can tell how much I give about
church attire these days) I really didn't come for this I simply just
came to serve/help the pastor. But, I couldn't deliberately be
disobedient even though I did want to.

You see I was already late to begin with, I left to go get the
fellow-ship pizza, was on my phone majority of the tutorial with
my yonibox sisters discussing last Friday's sinful epic fail moment
I had had. So, I had to go to the altar! A place I hadn't been in
years. I purposely let all the people go before me, had my purse
and my phone with me acting like someone was gone get my
stuff smdh. Simply trying to avoid the depths of what could
happen when one leaves things at the altar as I so often read in
the Bible. Honestly, just didn't want to feel anything or think of
anything I felt. Well long story short the bishop and his wife
begin to pray corporately, making declarations (law of
attraction), my mind is not on any of the law of attraction that's
being presented.

I'm leaping for joy thinking this the only prayer we having like a
little group. I was already nervous and uncomfortable being that
close anyways! Nope I was wrong! Now his wife has insisted he
lay hands on each of us individually. They was ready for warfare
on behalf of the people of God. To my luck they start on my end.
Here we go I'm thinking. As I try strongly to push all pain out of
my body, striving to remove any type of feelings I don't want to
attract or even think of (deep internalizing).

My adjutant training and knowledge desired to kick in but of
course I NEVER have a problem minding mines. I'm hoping he
wouldn't be able to see pain, fear or anything in me. Walking
around broken is my masterpiece. I've perfected the smile
behind the frown for a while now. Tears are hidden behind Red
eyes. and silence to avoid expression how I truly feel.

It's my turn the turn I didn't desire. The turn I didn't want. The
turn I was already nervous about is here! I can't run, I can't hide
I'm forced to participate in this moment. Well they start with the
forehead cross, (so this is when those raised in church know you

kinda raise your hands to show acceptance or give permission). So they start praying. In that moment a perfect stranger knew my life story and I had not uttered a word. Of course doubt creeps in (Hazel don't be stupid you know the last prophet that came for you studied your social media pages when you was in OceanSide he knew all about ya godmother who passed)

YEAH! I say to myself no tears sir I'm sure your a fraud like the others. Well little did I know God really was concerned about ya gurl. Jesus must've really been pleading for me. The Bishop hit home, picked my oracle card, read my palm and aligned my chakras in minutes. So, something again I hadn't done in a while I did on Friday the 13th, 2020 I recited the sinners prayer (Romans 10:9-13).

This time it felt different, it felt real, reassuring, refreshing, renewing, reviving. Ya girl saved. not perfect! But I do believe! My salvation might not fit into your customs or beliefs. Your traditions or your style. Your thoughts or your ways! But, guess what that's why it's my salvation. That's what makes me unique.

Let's aim to be less judge-mental during this martial law period we are in. Let's figure out how to really fellowship, and connect in kingdom-ship. Let's render more love than hate. Let's share our stories as testaments of redemption with the world. There is someone out there who needs your story and guess what it may look different from mines. Our TED talk may be different but ultimately the same if we speaking of the Trinity, The Messiah. Our differences shouldn't stop us from sharing our truth.

#COMPROMISE

I think some people do try it! A relationship with little to no compromise. One decided that being agreeable keeps things peaceful. So, purposely they neglect their actual feelings and input to ensure that their partner is happy. But, eventually this gets old. Love grows cold and the hearts suddenly begin to drift apart. Neither fully knowing what has lead to this end but both knowing it was for their good. Both still struggle with the issues faced. Compromise, honesty, empathy, support, understanding, judgement free zone. Really trying to see where they both went wrong. Hopeful to reunite but also hopeful this is actually OVER! Not sure if it was love or lust or did they actually love each other just unsure how to fully love due to the lack they each had for themselves. So, yes it's possible but the real question is was it or is it worth it? Compromise!

Thoughts & Scribble Sharing Time (use the next few pages to share your thoughts and unedited scribbles my hope) amorskies Life, a path we take daily with no knowledge of what to expect! We go endlessly with no understanding. Move in silence amongst a loud world. Confused by our vision. Grasping with purpose to our inner feels, wants, and desires. We must never stop reminding ourselves of who we are no matter what we face, or what others say about us, or too us! Growing confident with yourself doesn't make you less humble. It just give you strength to endure the wind. I AM who and what I say I AM 🖤 speaking richly over myself. I've alowed the outer voices to hold me hostage for to long. #BounceBackCold #BabyImGold #RichAsMyFather #UniqueSoul #LocDrivenGal #Humble&Confident #DestinedToSoar #Humble&Confident #Ready&Equipped #StrengthenedWithTenacity #LoveForgivenHealed #I Am #TheUnheard #StoryOfHope #JustCallMe #Hopeful

amorskies When I started this journey the excitement was overwhelming. I didn't know the stories or obstacles I'd face to complete it. But, in the end my passion for the Word of God (not traditions or customs) has flourished. I see things differently after studying deeply. I swear to you the spiritual journey is so much deeper than surface areas of scripture. It's deeper than a hop and hello. It's deeper than a sound and a step. Read it and I'm sure you'd stop your judging. If people would only actually invest more time in being knowledgeable verse being bold once a relationship with Christ should look like. We might have light in this dark world again. My thoughts, my opinion.
#TheUnheard #StoryOfHope #HopefulMonday #MyStory #MyHeart #MakeBelnPurpose #MakeAttention #AboutualOperation #StepJudging #StayRisiking #LearnRLove #Grow #idare #LTU #IHandleMOther #jowhi #Lift #OpenForSoul

amorskies You can't, you won't, it looks like it will NEVER happen for you. Words I've said to myself about me. She's a bad person, who does she think she is? Why is she even here? Words others have said about me. Well, truth is I'm me Flawed perfection! Graced beauty. Uniqued passion. Blessed wisdom. Purposed endurance. Blessed encouragement. So, take a moment to find perfection in your flaws today!

#RedLips #RedCup #RedSip #LasVegas #MDiv #Grad #ICelebration #Theology #LLC #Living #Learning #Growth #Celebrate #Birat-ion #TheStoryOf #UnheardHope #GrayLocs #MyJourney #MyStory #HerSmile #HerStrength #HerKiss #HerWish #Restored #Blissful #Courage #Wisdom

amorskies She stared at herself in a mirror. So many questions wandering through her mind. Confusion infused, and delusion consumed. Patiently letting something (to) cloud or scuds transpire in her life. The hurts runs deep, the pain cuts heavily, and her wounds push LOVE away. Is there one? Just like soul that can connect with a soul of brokenness? She's restless she's not one. So she decided she must learn to trust and wait for right to rediscover all save herself from the disaster she's already endures. #TransIpliedThursday #TransJentleman #Trustisawayoflife #TransPurgeEnri #TrustIsWayoutDfy #TrueJInsureStory #OfHope #HopeR,inuest #TueAlle

amorskies It was then she paused, and realized her worth. The moment she smiled she knew she was free from the hurt. The touch reached her soul. The kiss sparked new life. The passion created a pursuit of happiness. It was then, that very moment she became herself again. #Her #She #LoverOfLove #Ready #Pursuit #Trust #Vulnerable #Deep #Foreplay #SlowMotion #Laugh #Cry #WithMe #TheUnheardStoryOfHope #HopefulHazel #CanYou #LoveMePerfectly #Flawed #SoulTies #SoulfulLove #LoveSong #TakeMeAway #UckMySoul #Lifted #LocGoals #LocJourney #ColorPurposed

amorskies My eyes speak silently what the soul desires those close to hear. The whisper is like a facet leaking during a cold winter night. Ask me I promise I'll tell you no lies... #Eyes #Strength ##Courage #DreamingOfYou SelenasRedLip #Journey #UnheardHope

amorskies My balance back cold Strength in my bones like late growth. Mama said this would be the light of my life. I'm on gone steer no matter what tries to block me. Grandpa Bear's prayers being answered left and right. It's just grades baby! She may not watch her day routine? She daily matches the how to endure! My brother stone released his 5th album, text telling nothing he faces stop him! My love about to surprise the world with this magical project. My disciples are blossoming into some of the strongest women I've ever met. My grant (talives are blessed and amazing. Me and friend can't be stopped at back and watch us all low. Yet shit, I'm not at rest as I stand at self as I seen. I'm not a stepping stool, I'm a pitval possession. Just watch how if she fall to rise I've a fault mind and old black ish but if your miserable agenda you consent or negative methods. Man about a life if you u same ass a blike. Not prophetic but will call Mexican girl why seek out Justice! Jean a New and Lit baps to (get I'm blues blues. Jogs #RichJahnoun #lee #lag #HopeEnce #Ilifing #Blogging,ry, ls #Itishcam #Lunhe

amorskies I'm just a hopeful gal full of passion who refuses to settle for the bullshit she once accepted. I got lost a little but trust and believe I've been found 💯 🖤 #UnheardHope #HopefulHazel #iAm #TheUnheardStory #OfHope #locsroc #GirlsWithLocsRoc #LocJourney #ILoveMyLocs #IBlog #BloggerLife #MyStory #MyJourney #MyWorld #MyUtopia #SeeThroughMyEyes www.unheardhope.com

amorskies I see the depths of a soul, feel the vibes of the cold. Listen to the silent voice. Understand the distant presence. Conflicted thoughts often translated through intimacy. Lack of trust as words are lies. I am like a goddess of bountiful blessings. Strengthened with divine purpose. Caught by the hand of God each time I fall. #WCW #ME #HAZEL #THE #UNHEARD #STORY #OF #HOPE #CALL #ME #HOPEFUL #LOCS #GREY #GRAY #WISDOM #MY #JOURNEY #MY #STORY #ALIVE #DRYBONES #ARISE #NEW #LIFE #TRY #AGAIN #BOUNCE #BACK #COLD #SOLID #READY #VICTORIOUS #WINNER

amorskies The moment SHE released SHE grew free 🖤 www.unheardhope.com

amorskies Them: your lips are so big. Are your eyes black? What happened to your chin? Why you so mad? Bihhhh do you ever smile? Her: my lips are perfect. Nobody has black eyes stupid. Life happened to this unique chin. Ain't nobody mad but the devil ole goofy ask. Honestly you couldn't handle my smile. #iamTheUnheardStoryOfHope #HopefulHazel #YeahThatsMe #LocGirl #LocUpdo #ThatOneNight #InTheAzHeat #Living #Loving #Learning

amorskies it was in that moment I valued me. I accepted every flaw, embraced every scar, and acknowledged that the sniff of a rose held the healing serum for my soul! #NewBlogAlert #Blogger #iBlog #My 🖤 DesiresPeace #iAm #TheUnheardStoryOfHope #MyChaos #MyChronicles #MyJourney #MyChapter34 #UpsDowns #HighsLows #Ready #Stronger #Better #Wiser #Unique #OnlyCanBeMe #LoveMe #HateMe #JustWanna #GetWastedOffYou www.unheardhope.com 🖤

amorskies: ... was in that moment she knew even when the fire was on every side of her she had no fear and would survive. So she screamed, gasped for air then smiled and laughed. Wow! The God of all truly never lets her fall. 🖤

amorskies It's when I look up I feel your presence, I hear your voice, I smell you near. Lost in the now crazy about the future and ready for today like Never before. Free to LOVE you with every ounce of my soul. Lost in your love language just patiently waiting for you to come home🖤 #TheStory #Of #UnheardHope #SheThoughtIt #SoSheBecame #Strength2HerSoul #Life2HerBones #2019 #Vibes #Ready #Bright #LocsLove #GlowUp #Glam #Ready #Fighter #Survivor #Peace #Happy #Breathing #Saved

amorskies She will take you into undiscovered worlds of mystery and magic. She will lead you, mesmerized and half-drunk with love, into the wild forests of sensual ecstasy and wonder. #AwakenedAmor 😈 💯 🤍

October 23, 2017

amorskies 🤍 full of chaos but I'll still 👀 your mind with my 🤍

December 14, 2017

amorskies I got dressed for church yesterday. Pulled up and couldn't get out of my truck! Idk if I was fearful of being in a room of those who attacked my character. Or if I was angry that someone could possibly be praying, preaching, speaking in tongues but can't simply apologize for 🤍 n me over! Either or long story short LMBO I was cute as hell but Sunday service just wasn't a for me! 💯🤍 🙏🏽🙌🏽 not a judgmental person I never have been and never desire to be but somethings that have occurred in the course of my 30s got me questioning everything smdh LMBO

amorskies Truth is I've spent damn near 7 months wishing they would hurt like they hurt me! But today I forgive them, simply because they never even knew me if they did they would've never hurt me! The good news is I know me and who I'm becoming without their using behavior, betrayal, backstabbing, gossip, and lies in my life. I'm thankful I'm learning to wear LOVE and not HATE! God forgives and I must do the same moving on into a joyful place in my life! Keep talking ITCHES 😂 idgaf about what you got to say anymore. They thought they would break me, but I'm still standing B! They thought they could destroy my character but I'm rising above it all B! My only regret in life was TRUSTING them but my guy won't be discombobulated by the betrayal of them! I am officially FREE from IT ALL! At the end of the day what I think of me matters most 🔑 the rest. 💯🤍 #TheStoryOfUnheardHope #JustCallMeHopeful #GotMySmileBack

amorskies I've won, I've lost, I've cried, I've laughed, I've been through HELL with HEAVEN on my side! Strength of a woman. Gifted by the hand of God. Stronger because of the pain. I've learned to gain wisdom you must first release any and everything that means you no good. It wasn't the plan to loose but it was the plan to recover even through the loss. #UnheardHope #CallMeHopeful 💯🤍 #tbt #StillBlessed 😈🤍

amorskies Sometimes laughing through the pain is all you can do. Protecting you is one of the most important keys to success! Take the risk but do it silently even the ones who broke bread with Jesus denied Him. Don't give strangers, family so called friends access to you heart! I learned the hard way and that 🔑 will never happen again! Life is all about living, learning, and growing! Stay focused no matter how dark and painful this journey maybe! When folks try to destroy you publicly simply because they can't understand you God will always prepare a table in front of your enemies! No need to respond in foot pray for them and watch God change things in you life! It took me a while to get here because I got sick of being attacked, lied on, and judged by church idiots LOL. But once I realized who I am their opinions of me never will matter again! #Stronger #Wiser #Growing I don't need your pulpit to do the work of the Lord! I can keep my hard earned money and sow into areas that really need it encourage and uplift individuals who really want something out of the asides from leading a broken congregation that on has a form of godliness and forever will deny the power. I'm coo off they setting! There are millions of people who have never heard of the name Jesus, and you think time sit around an argue w you about some denominations foolishness, a random title and position, my attire and lipstick! Next my love may not be perfect but trust me my heart is pure! And I believe Jesus saves, redeems, and frees 🤍🙏🏽🙌🏽

amorskies As the world began to spin she stood still in the silence wondering how fast life was trying to pass her bye. Gasping for air, reaching up to the sky, and dreaming to escape from the agony that's crippled her soul. But through it all she defeated defeat and survived the crash of when her heart dropped to earth to discover the true divine purpose of her needed presence 🤍

Edited · 195w

amorskies Drifting in the battlefield of my mind. So consumed with the pressures of this world, longing for an escape. Be my escape baby. Hold me, grip me, rub me, feed my soul with your knowledge and wisdom. Ignite the fire of passion since my flame has been deemed out. Restore my jubilance with vibrant colors. Love me back to life. - 🤍 Self

amorskies Sometimes the pause and the stare are reminders why I chose not to 🤍 with those who mean me no good! I see you even when you think I'm not watching. I hear you even when you think I'm not listening. I'm wiser than your stupidity of betrayal and in the end I'll always WIN! 💯🤍

amorskies Sometimes I get lost in my own silence. Listening to the sound of the wind blowing through my hang time. As I laugh at my secret jokes while starring in the eyes of my eyes. Through the reflection of the camera facing me. Allowing me to drift away but for a moment as I so desire to be lost in my hope. Surrounded by the touch of earth breathing such frequencies of peace. Capturing the dull moments with memories recited from my soul. Of past loves and experiences I wish daily I could have back. I'm just the unheard story of hope. A girl that's free 💯🤍

amorskies She starred at the reflection of herself. She could see the hurt, betrayal, the lies, the open wounds, and even the brokenness. Then someone asked her how she's able to do it. Her response in a soft tone it's not me who does it, it's Him! Without Him I would of ended it long ago 🤍💯 #UnheardStoryOfHope #JustCallMeHopeful

View all 2 comments

April 6, 2018

Story of HOPE

Chapter 12: The Season of Bipolar Scribbles

Some people have a season in your life while others are meant for eternity We go way back to births of kiddos to drunken fights downtown ABQ! Needless to say the many ghetto moments on 2nd St. To worthless marriages in our early 20s. To depression battles, lost souls seeking their deeper purpose in life to being rays of light and beginning to recognize the inner goddess' we are as we've traveled into our 30s. All I can say is my bestfriend is so much better than yours I never knew someone could love me through my good and bad, accept me in my trauma stages of still stand with me in the healing days of my life. Thankful for you sis. I'm so grateful that even when we don't agree we agree that our friendship matters regardless, and we have the ability to move on. I lost a marriage you were there! You lost a marriage I was there. I lost a child you were there! You had a child I was there! I lost my brother you were there! Moms and that damn cancer I was there! See no matter what was happening in our lives we were there! Thank you for being there! Thank you for my namesake "Ja'Hazel" thank you for my god children. Thank you for your strength and sometimes overpowering confidence! Thank you for being you a true Ryder that's had my back in some deep rooted ugly situations. I may not say it enough bestfriend but I love you, I thank God for you. My prayer for you this 35th year of life is that no matter what YOU NEVER GIVE UP! That when the days are low NEVER GIVE UP! That when your anxiety attacks you fight & NEVER GIVE UP! May you forever know the Ase' Power you carry and know that I am here and will support, encourage, uplift and correct you forever my bestfriend. i love you bestfriend.

#TheStory #OfUnheard #Hope #NuBlog #Finally #MyBestfriend #SheBetter #ThanYours #Sisters #Life #Growth #RealFriendships #Truthful #Praying #Encouraging

#Bond #QuarantineBlog #LongOverDue #MayWriteAnother
#241#TheStory #OfUnheard #Hope #NuBlog #Finally
#MyBestfriend #SheBetter #ThanYours #Sisters #Life
#Growth #RealFriendships #Truthful #Praying #Encouraging
#Bond #QuarantineBlog #LongOverDue #MayWriteAnother
#241

LOST FILES: NOVEMBER 2019

Day before thanksgiving thankful thoughts with Hopeful Hazel
(tomorrow I'll be busy ceLIVEbrate'n). Well I'm thankful for
surviving the disaster, overcoming the mess, relinquishing the
bitterness, letting go of anger, finding peace, a self healing
journey (with its highs and lows), accomplishing goals/dreams, a
go getter mind mentality, balance, self awareness, self respect,
self love, healthy grief (even w/o support). For years I've catered
to everyone. Cared for others more than I've cared for myself.
Held on to relationships that were literally toxic for the sake of
being in one. But when I awakened saw myself in the reflection
of the glass that I held to my lips (Beyonce voice). I saw
brokenness, I saw a girl not a woman taunted by the hurt and
abuse of her past. I refuse to carry any dead weight into MY new
century. If my bubble keeps getting smaller I'll continue to be
thankful. I'm not perfect I'm for damn sure flawed but what I do
know now that I didn't know then is WHO TF I AM #Period't
and that my Hopes is the best feeling ever. Knowing WHO you
are and WHOSE you are are huge in this journey. When you
realize WHO YOU are you stop accepting and allowing certain
things to enter into your presence. When you know WHOSE
YOU ARE you refrain from wasting energy and time. You even
tend to respond differently as only ONE opinion of you truly
matters. It took me sometime but honey when I tell you I'm

thankful for the process as it's producing a wise woman who will forever be thankful throughout her journey, and will remain full of hope. I am the Unheard Story Of Hope

ASE' ASE' ASE'

Ase' I AM! I AM WHO I AM! Hopeful Hazel, a Bipolar Aquarius, A Omnist, A Healer, A Spiritualist, A Chakra Aligner, A Helpmate, A Server, A Shoulder, A Ray of Hope, A Visionary, A Prophetic Oracle, A Card Reader, A Goddess, A Queen, A Woman, A sHero, A Friend, A Judgement Free Zone, I Am The Unheard Story of Hope. Stay tune my HOPES vol.2 will be filled with even more of my random UNEDITED thoughts and scribbles or at least I think....

Freedom Day Last Day of Residency for
Mdiv. 2019

CPSIA information can be obtained
at www.ICGtesting.com
Printed in the USA
BVHW060844160721
612126BV00022B/1489